50% OFF Online Social Work ASWB Masters Prep Course!

Dear Customer,

We consider it an honor and a privilege that you chose our LMSW Study Guide. As a way of showing our appreciation and to help us better serve you, we have partnered with Mometrix Test Preparation to offer you **50% off their online Social Work ASWB Masters Prep Course**. Many LMSW courses are needlessly expensive and don't deliver enough value. With their course, you get access to the best LMSW prep material, and **you only pay half price**.

Mometrix has structured their online course to perfectly complement your workbook. The LMSW Prep Course contains **in-depth lessons** that cover all the most important topics, **30+ video reviews** that explain difficult concepts, over **1,000 practice questions** to ensure you feel prepared, and more than **440 digital flashcards**, so you can study while you're on the go.

Online Social Work ASWB Masters Prep Course

Topics Included:

- Human Development, Diversity, and Behavior in the Environment
- Assessment and Intervention Planning
- Interventions with Clients/Client Systems
- Professional Relationships, Values, and Ethics

Course Features:

- LMSW Study Guide
    - Get content that complements our best-selling study guide.
- Full-Length Practice Tests
    - With over 1,000 practice questions, you can test yourself again and again.
- Mobile Friendly
    - If you need to study on the go, the course is easily accessible from your mobile device.
- LMSW Flashcards
    - Our course includes a flashcard mode with over 440 content cards to help you study.

To receive this discount, visit them at mometrix.com/university/aswbm/ or simply scan this QR code with your smartphone. At the checkout page, enter the discount code: **LMSW50TPB**

If you have any questions or concerns, please contact them at support@mometrix.com.

Sincerely,

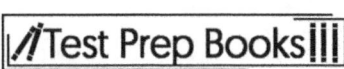 in partnership with

Online Resources

We host multiple bonus items online, including a customizable prep plan and a convenient study timer to help you manage your time.

Go to the last page of this book to find the instructions to access these resources.

LMSW Companion Workbook 2025-2026
Fill-in-the-Blank Study Guide Companion for ASWB Masters Exam Prep and Practice

Lydia Morrison

Copyright © 2025 by TPB Publishing

All rights reserved. No part of this publication may be reproduced, distributed, or transmitted in any form or by any means, including photocopying, recording, or other electronic or mechanical methods, without the prior written permission of the publisher, except in the case of brief quotations embodied in critical reviews and certain other noncommercial uses permitted by copyright law.

Written and edited by TPB Publishing.

TPB Publishing is not associated with or endorsed by any official testing organization. TPB Publishing is a publisher of unofficial educational products. All test and organization names are trademarks of their respective owners. Content in this book is included for utilitarian purposes only and does not constitute an endorsement by TPB Publishing of any particular point of view.

Interested in buying more than 10 copies of our product? Contact us about bulk discounts:
bulkorders@studyguideteam.com

ISBN 13: 9781637757246

Table of Contents

Welcome -- 1
How to Use This Product -- 2
Quick Overview --- 3
Test-Taking Strategies --- 4
Introduction to the ASWB Masters Exam -- 8
Human Development, Diversity and Behavior in the Environment --- 12
    Human Growth and Development --- 12
    Concepts of Abuse and Neglect -- 35
    Diversity, Social/Economic Justice, and Oppression --------------------- 36
Assessment and Intervention Planning ------------------------------------ 40
    Biopsychosocial History and Collateral Data ---------------------------- 40
    Assessment Methods and Techniques -------------------------------------- 48
    Intervention Planning -- 57
Interventions with Clients/Client System -------------------------------- 59
    Intervention Processes and Techniques for Use Across Systems ----------- 59
    Intervention Processed and Techniques for Use with Larger Systems ------ 68
Professional Relationships, Values, and Ethics -------------------------- 73
    Professional Values and Ethical Issues --------------------------------- 73
    Confidentiality -- 78
    Professional Development and Use of Self ------------------------------- 78
Online Resources -- 85

Welcome

Dear Reader,

Welcome to your new Test Prep Books workbook. We are pleased that you chose us to help you prepare for your exam. There are many study options to choose from, and we appreciate you choosing us. Studying can be a daunting task, but we have designed a smart, effective study guide to help prepare you for what lies ahead.

Whether you're a parent helping your child learn and grow, a high school student working hard to get into your dream college, or a nursing student studying for a complex exam, we want to help give you the tools you need to succeed. We hope this study guide gives you the skills and the confidence to thrive, and we can't thank you enough for allowing us to be part of your journey.

In an effort to continue to improve our products, we welcome feedback from our customers. We look forward to hearing from you. Suggestions, success stories, and criticisms can all be communicated by emailing us at info@studyguideteam.com.

Sincerely,
Test Prep Books Team

How to Use This Product

This book is designed to be used in conjunction with our LMSW study guide to help you prepare for the ASWB Masters exam. As you go through each section of the study guide, use this book to take notes and highlight key concepts in a way that best helps you to understand and engage with the material. Whether you're learning the material for the first time or reviewing it, the goal of this workbook is to help you take meaningful notes and retain critical information so that you feel confident and prepared on exam day.

Quick Overview

As you draw closer to taking your exam, effective preparation becomes more and more important. Thankfully, you have this workbook to help you get ready. Use this guide to help keep your studying on track and refer to it often.

Also included are test-taking tips. Knowing the right information is not always enough. Many well-prepared test takers struggle with exams. These tips will help equip you to accurately read, assess, and answer test questions.

Don't try to cram the night before you take your exam. This is not a wise strategy for a few reasons. First, your retention of the information will be low. Your time would be better used by reviewing information you already know rather than trying to learn a lot of new information. Second, you will likely become stressed as you try to gain a large amount of knowledge in a short amount of time. Third, you will be depriving yourself of sleep. So be sure to go to bed at a reasonable time the night before. Being well-rested helps you focus and remain calm.

Be sure to eat a substantial breakfast the morning of the exam. If you are taking the exam in the afternoon, be sure to have a good lunch as well. Being hungry is distracting and can make it difficult to focus. You have hopefully spent lots of time preparing for the exam. Don't let an empty stomach get in the way of success!

When travelling to the testing center, leave earlier than needed. That way, you have a buffer in case you experience any delays. This will help you remain calm and will keep you from missing your appointment time at the testing center.

Be sure to pace yourself during the exam. Don't try to rush through the exam. There is no need to risk performing poorly on the exam just so you can leave the testing center early. Allow yourself to use all of the allotted time if needed.

Remain positive while taking the exam even if you feel like you are performing poorly. Thinking about the content you should have mastered will not help you perform better on the exam.

Once the exam is complete, take some time to relax. Even if you feel that you need to take the exam again, you will be well served by some down time before you begin studying again. It's often easier to convince yourself to study if you know that it will come with a reward!

Test-Taking Strategies

1. Predicting the Answer

When you feel confident in your preparation for a multiple-choice test, try predicting the answer before reading the answer choices. This is especially useful on questions that test objective factual knowledge. By predicting the answer before reading the available choices, you eliminate the possibility that you will be distracted or led astray by an incorrect answer choice. You will feel more confident in your selection if you read the question, predict the answer, and then find your prediction among the answer choices. After using this strategy, be sure to still read all of the answer choices carefully and completely. If you feel unprepared, you should not attempt to predict the answers. This would be a waste of time and an opportunity for your mind to wander in the wrong direction.

2. Reading the Whole Question

Too often, test takers scan a multiple-choice question, recognize a few familiar words, and immediately jump to the answer choices. Test authors are aware of this common impatience, and they will sometimes prey upon it. For instance, a test author might subtly turn the question into a negative, or he or she might redirect the focus of the question right at the end. The only way to avoid falling into these traps is to read the entirety of the question carefully before reading the answer choices.

3. Looking for Wrong Answers

Long and complicated multiple-choice questions can be intimidating. One way to simplify a difficult multiple-choice question is to eliminate all of the answer choices that are clearly wrong. In most sets of answers, there will be at least one selection that can be dismissed right away. If the test is administered on paper, the test taker could draw a line through it to indicate that it may be ignored; otherwise, the test taker will have to perform this operation mentally or on scratch paper. In either case, once the obviously incorrect answers have been eliminated, the remaining choices may be considered. Sometimes identifying the clearly wrong answers will give the test taker some information about the correct answer. For instance, if one of the remaining answer choices is a direct opposite of one of the eliminated answer choices, it may well be the correct answer. The opposite of obviously wrong is obviously right! Of course, this is not always the case. Some answers are obviously incorrect simply because they are irrelevant to the question being asked. Still, identifying and eliminating some incorrect answer choices is a good way to simplify a multiple-choice question.

4. Don't Overanalyze

Anxious test takers often overanalyze questions. When you are nervous, your brain will often run wild, causing you to make associations and discover clues that don't actually exist. If you feel that this may be a problem for you, do whatever you can to slow down during the test. Try taking a deep breath or counting to ten. As you read and consider the question, restrict yourself to the particular words used by the author. Avoid thought tangents about what the author *really* meant, or what he or she was *trying* to say. The only things that matter on a multiple-choice test are the words that are actually in the question. You must avoid reading too much into a multiple-choice question, or supposing that the writer meant something other than what he or she wrote.

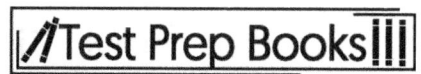

5. No Need for Panic

It is wise to learn as many strategies as possible before taking a multiple-choice test, but it is likely that you will come across a few questions for which you simply don't know the answer. In this situation, avoid panicking. Because most multiple-choice tests include dozens of questions, the relative value of a single wrong answer is small. As much as possible, you should compartmentalize each question on a multiple-choice test. In other words, you should not allow your feelings about one question to affect your success on the others. When you find a question that you either don't understand or don't know how to answer, just take a deep breath and do your best. Read the entire question slowly and carefully. Try rephrasing the question a couple of different ways. Then, read all of the answer choices carefully. After eliminating obviously wrong answers, make a selection and move on to the next question.

6. Confusing Answer Choices

When working on a difficult multiple-choice question, there may be a tendency to focus on the answer choices that are the easiest to understand. Many people, whether consciously or not, gravitate to the answer choices that require the least concentration, knowledge, and memory. This is a mistake. When you come across an answer choice that is confusing, you should give it extra attention. A question might be confusing because you do not know the subject matter to which it refers. If this is the case, don't

eliminate the answer before you have affirmatively settled on another. When you come across an answer choice of this type, set it aside as you look at the remaining choices. If you can confidently assert that one of the other choices is correct, you can leave the confusing answer aside. Otherwise, you will need to take a moment to try to better understand the confusing answer choice. Rephrasing is one way to tease out the sense of a confusing answer choice.

7. Your First Instinct

Many people struggle with multiple-choice tests because they overthink the questions. If you have studied sufficiently for the test, you should be prepared to trust your first instinct once you have carefully and completely read the question and all of the answer choices. There is a great deal of research suggesting that the mind can come to the correct conclusion very quickly once it has obtained all of the relevant information. At times, it may seem to you as if your intuition is working faster even than your reasoning mind. This may in fact be true. The knowledge you obtain while studying may be retrieved from your subconscious before you have a chance to work out the associations that support it. Verify your instinct by working out the reasons that it should be trusted.

8. Key Words

Many test takers struggle with multiple-choice questions because they have poor reading comprehension skills. Quickly reading and understanding a multiple-choice question requires a mixture of skill and experience. To help with this, try jotting down a few key words and phrases on a piece of scrap paper. Doing this concentrates the process of reading and forces the mind to weigh the relative importance of the question's parts. In selecting words and phrases to write down, the test taker thinks about the question more deeply and carefully. This is especially true for multiple-choice questions that are preceded by a long prompt.

9. Subtle Negatives

One of the oldest tricks in the multiple-choice test writer's book is to subtly reverse the meaning of a question with a word like *not* or *except*. If you are not paying attention to each word in the question, you can easily be led astray by this trick. For instance, a common question format is, "Which of the following is...?" Obviously, if the question instead is, "Which of the following is not...?," then the answer will be quite different. Even worse, the test makers are aware of the potential for this mistake and will include one answer choice that would be correct if the question were not negated or reversed. A test taker who misses the reversal will find what he or she believes to be a correct answer and will be so confident that he or she will fail to reread the question and discover the original error. The only way to avoid this is to practice a wide variety of multiple-choice questions and to pay close attention to each and every word.

10. Reading Every Answer Choice

It may seem obvious, but you should always read every one of the answer choices! Too many test takers fall into the habit of scanning the question and assuming that they understand the question because they recognize a few key words. From there, they pick the first answer choice that answers the question they believe they have read. Test takers who read all of the answer choices might discover that one of the latter answer choices is actually *more* correct. Moreover, reading all of the answer choices can remind you of facts related to the question that can help you arrive at the correct answer. Sometimes, a misstatement or incorrect detail in one of the latter answer choices will trigger your memory of the subject and will enable you to find the right answer. Failing to read all of the answer choices is like not reading all of the items on a restaurant menu: you might miss out on the perfect choice.

11. Spot the Hedges

One of the keys to success on multiple-choice tests is paying close attention to every word. This is never truer than with words like *almost*, *most*, *some*, and *sometimes*. These words are called "hedges" because they indicate that a statement is not totally true or not true in every place and time. An absolute statement will contain no hedges, but in many subjects, the answers are not always straightforward or absolute. There are always exceptions to the rules in these subjects. For this reason,

you should favor those multiple-choice questions that contain hedging language. The presence of qualifying words indicates that the author is taking special care with his or her words, which is certainly important when composing the right answer. After all, there are many ways to be wrong, but there is only one way to be right! For this reason, it is wise to avoid answers that are absolute when taking a multiple-choice test. An absolute answer is one that says things are either all one way or all another. They often include words like *every*, *always*, *best*, and *never*. If you are taking a multiple-choice test in a subject that doesn't lend itself to absolute answers, be on your guard if you see any of these words.

Test-Taking Strategies

12. Long Answers

In many subject areas, the answers are not simple. As already mentioned, the right answer often requires hedges. Another common feature of the answers to a complex or subjective question are qualifying clauses, which are groups of words that subtly modify the meaning of the sentence. If the question or answer choice describes a rule to which there are exceptions or the subject matter is complicated, ambiguous, or confusing, the correct answer will require many words in order to be expressed clearly and accurately. In essence, you should not be deterred by answer choices that seem excessively long. Oftentimes, the author of the text will not be able to write the correct answer without offering some qualifications and modifications. Your job is to read the answer choices thoroughly and completely and to select the one that most accurately and precisely answers the question.

13. Restating to Understand

Sometimes, a question on a multiple-choice test is difficult not because of what it asks but because of how it is written. If this is the case, restate the question or answer choice in different words. This process serves a couple of important purposes. First, it forces you to concentrate on the core of the question. In order to rephrase the question accurately, you have to understand it well. Rephrasing the question will concentrate your mind on the key words and ideas. Second, it will present the information to your mind in a fresh way. This process may trigger your memory and render some useful scrap of information picked up while studying.

14. True Statements

Sometimes an answer choice will be true in itself, but it does not answer the question. This is one of the main reasons why it is essential to read the question carefully and completely before proceeding to the answer choices. Too often, test takers skip ahead to the answer choices and look for true statements. Having found one of these, they are content to select it without reference to the question above. The savvy test taker will always read the entire question before turning to the answer choices. Then, having settled on a correct answer choice, he or she will refer to the original question and ensure that the selected answer is relevant. The mistake of choosing a correct-but-irrelevant answer choice is especially common on questions related to specific pieces of objective knowledge.

15. No Patterns

One of the more dangerous ideas that circulates about multiple-choice tests is that the correct answers tend to fall into patterns. These erroneous ideas range from a belief that B and C are the most common right answers, to the idea that an unprepared test-taker should answer "A-B-A-C-A-D-A-B-A." It cannot be emphasized enough that pattern-seeking of this type is exactly the WRONG way to approach a multiple-choice test. To begin with, it is highly unlikely that the test maker will plot the correct answers according to some predetermined pattern. The questions are scrambled and delivered in a random order. Furthermore, even if the test maker was following a pattern in the assignation of correct answers, there is no reason why the test taker would know which pattern he or she was using. Any attempt to discern a pattern in the answer choices is a waste of time and a distraction from the real work of taking the test. A test taker would be much better served by extra preparation before the test than by reliance on a pattern in the answers.

7

Introduction to the ASWB Masters Exam

Function of the Test

An Association of Social Work Boards (ASWB) Master's exam is used for licensure as a master social worker, or the equivalent, in all fifty U.S. states as well as the District of Columbia, the U.S. Virgin Islands, Alberta, and British Columbia. The Master's exam is typically taken by a new graduate of a master's degree program in social work as part of the licensing process, but can also be taken by someone already in the field with an eye toward a new or upgraded license.

In 2016, 15,442 people took the ASWB Master's exam, and 81.2 percent of those test takers passed. The passing score is determined nationally, and not on a state-by-state or board-by-board basis.

Test Administration

ASWB exams are given by computer. They are not administered on any particular fixed dates. Instead, tests are given by appointment at Pearson Professional Centers worldwide. Students must first register for the test, then visit Pearson VUE's website to schedule an exam sitting.

Candidates with disabilities can receive appropriate accommodations while taking the ASWB Master's exam by applying for accommodations through the ASWB website. Candidates whose first language is not English can also seek arrangements for alternate language exams in most jurisdictions.

Candidates must wait 90 days before retaking the exam, although exceptions can be made when there is a serious, documented malfunction with the initial attempt, or if employment is at stake and the initial score was within five correct answers of passing.

Test Format

Each examination lasts four hours and contains 170 four-option, multiple-choice questions in four categories of practice. 150 of the 170 items are scored, while the remainder is used for test validation purposes. Candidates have four hours to complete the electronically administered test.

The four categories of practice for the Master's exam are as follows: Human Development, Diversity, and Behavior in the Environment; Assessment and Intervention Planning; Interventions with Clients/Client Systems; and Professional Relationships, Values, and Ethics. Each section comprises roughly one quarter of the exam. Details are contained in the Knowledge, Skills, and Abilities statement (KSA) published by ASWB.

Here's a table of the sections:

Category	Subcategories	% of Exam
Human Development, Diversity, and Behavior in the Environment	Human Growth and Development	27%
	Concepts of Abuse and Neglect	
	Diversity, Social/Economic Justice, and Oppression	
Assessment and Intervention Planning	Biopsychosocial History and Collateral Data	24%
	Assessment Methods and Techniques	
	Intervention Planning	
Interventions with Clients/Client Systems	Intervention Processes and Techniques for Use Across Systems	24%
	Intervention Processes and Techniques for Use with Larger Systems	
Professional Relationships, Values, and Ethics	Professional Values and Ethical Issues	25%
	Confidentiality	
	Professional Development and Use of Self	

Scoring

Like all ASWB exams, the Master's exam is scored pass/fail, with a certain number of correct answers required in order to pass. The pass point varies from exam to exam based on the difficulty of a given test, but it generally ranges somewhere between 93 and 107 correct answers out of 150 scored questions. There is no penalty for guessing, as the total number of correct answers is the only factor in a test taker's raw score.

Although different states and jurisdictions have different numbers in their rules as a required passing score, the performance required to pass the exam is actually no higher or lower in any one state than in any other. Instead, the score reported by ASWB to each state is scaled to that state's required score. In

other words, a test taker who gets exactly the score needed to pass nationally would have that score reported as a 70 in a state that requires a 70 to pass, and reported as a 75 in a state that requires a 75 to pass.

Recent/Future Developments

The content of the ASWB exams is constantly being updated to incorporate new information from the field of social work, such as changes in the new *DSM-5-TR*. However, no other structural or testing procedure changes have been announced for the immediate future.

As you study for your test, we'd like to take the opportunity to remind you that you are capable of great things! With the right tools and dedication, you truly can do anything you set your mind to. The fact that you are holding this book right now shows how committed you are. In case no one has told you lately, you've got this! Our intention behind including this coloring page is to give you the chance to take some time to engage your creative side when you need a little brain-break from studying. As a company, we want to encourage people like you to achieve their dreams by providing good quality study materials for the tests and certifications that improve careers and change lives. As individuals, many of us have taken such tests in our careers, and we know how challenging this process can be. While we can't come alongside you and cheer you on personally, we can offer you the space to recall your purpose, reconnect with your passion, and refresh your brain through an artistic practice. We wish you every success, and happy studying!

Human Development, Diversity and Behavior in the Environment

Human Growth and Development

Human Development Throughout the Lifespan

<u>Sigmund Freud</u>

Stages of Psychosexual Development:

1.) _____

  - _____
  - _____
  - _____

2.) _____

  - _____
  - _____
  - _____

3.) _____

  - _____
  - _____

4.) _____

  - _____
  - _____
  - _____

5.) _____

  - _____
  - _____
  - _____

<u>Erik Erikson</u>

Models of Psychosocial Development:

1.) _____

  - _____
  - _____

2.) _____

  - _____
  - _____
  - _____

Human Development, Diversity and Behavior in the Environment

3.) _____

- _____
- _____
- _____

4.) _____

- _____
- _____
- _____

5.) _____

- _____
- _____
- _____

6.) _____

- _____
- _____
- _____

7.) _____

- _____
- _____
- _____

8.) _____

- _____
- _____
- _____

Jean Piaget

Terms to Know:

Assimilation:
_____
_____
_____

Accommodation:
_____
_____
_____

Schemas:
_____
_____
_____

Stages of Cognitive Development:

1.) _____

- _____
- _____
- _____
- _____

2.) _____

- _____

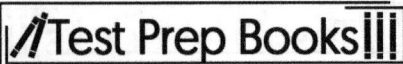

Human Development, Diversity and Behavior in the Environment

- _____
- _____

3.) _____

- _____
- _____
- _____

4.) _____

- _____
- _____
- _____
- _____

Ivan Pavlov

_____
_____
_____

Terms to Know:

Classical conditioning:
_____
_____
_____

B.F. Skinner

Terms to Know:

Operant conditioning:
_____
_____
_____

Positive reinforcement:
_____
_____
_____
_____

Negative reinforcement:
_____
_____
_____
_____

Punishment:
_____
_____
_____

Superstition:
_____
_____
_____

Shaping:
_____
_____
_____

Skinner's schedules of reinforcement:

1.) _____

2.) _____

3.) _____

Human Development, Diversity and Behavior in the Environment

4.) _____

5.) _____

6.) _____

Daniel Levinson

Seasons of Life Theory

1.) _____

- _____

2.) _____

- _____

3.) _____

- _____

4.) _____

- _____

5.) _____

- _____

6.) _____

- _____

Bernice Neugarten

Social Clock Theory:

Normal and Abnormal Physical, Cognitive, Emotional, and Sexual Development Throughout the Lifespan

Developmental milestones:

Infancy through age five:

School age to adolescence:

Adolescence:

Terms to Know:

Cognitive development:

Zone of proximal development:

Social development:

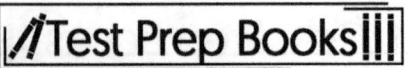

Human Development, Diversity and Behavior in the Environment

Social learning:
_____
_____
_____

Emotional development:
_____
_____
_____

Normal behaviors:
_____
_____
_____

Abnormal behaviors:
_____
_____
_____

DSM-5-TR:
_____
_____
_____

Commonly recognized milestones in early cognitive development:
- _____
  _____
  _____

- _____
  _____
  _____

- _____
  _____
  _____

- _____
  _____
  _____

- _____
  _____
  _____

- _____
  _____
  _____

What can caregivers do to support positive social development?

- _____
  _____
  _____

- _____
  _____
  _____

- _____
  _____
  _____

- _____
  _____
  _____

- _____
  _____
  _____

Lev Vygotsky
_____
_____
_____

Human Development, Diversity and Behavior in the Environment

Examples of positive emotional growth and development in children:

- _____
- _____
- _____
- _____
- _____
- _____
- _____
- _____
- _____

- _____
- _____

Terms to Know:

Sexually-reactive child:
_____

Consciousness:
_____

Pre-consciousness:
_____

Unconsciousness:
_____

Id:
_____

Thanatos:
_____

Eros:
_____

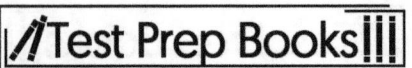

Human Development, Diversity and Behavior in the Environment

Libido:
_____
_____
_____

Ego:
_____
_____
_____

Superego:
_____
_____
_____

Ego strength:
_____
_____
_____

Spiritual Development Throughout the Lifespan

Terms to Know:

Spiritual development:
_____
_____
_____

Jean Piaget (1927-1987)
_____
_____
_____
_____
_____

Lawrence Kohlberg (1927-1987)
_____
_____
_____
_____

James Fowler (1940-2015)
_____
_____
_____
_____

Racial, Ethnic, and Cultural Development Throughout the Lifespan

Jean Kim's theory of Asian racial identity development:
_____
_____
_____
_____

Bernardo Ferdman and Placida Gallego's Model of Latino Identity Development
_____
_____
_____
_____

Physical, Mental, and Cognitive Disabilities Throughout the Lifespan
_____
_____
_____
_____
_____
_____
_____
_____
_____

Human Development, Diversity and Behavior in the Environment

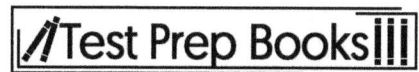

Interplay of Biological, Psychological, Social, and Spiritual Factors

_____
_____
_____
_____
_____
_____
_____

Basic Human Needs

Abraham Maslow

_____
_____
_____
_____

Fill out Maslow's Hierarchy of Needs:

Use this space to fill out more details about Maslow's Hierarchy of Needs:

- _____
- _____
- _____
- _____
- _____
- _____

Attachment and Bonding

Words to know:

Bonding: _____
_____

Human Development, Diversity and Behavior in the Environment

Attachment:

Avoidant attachment:

Ambivalent attachment:

Effects of Aging on Biopsychosocial Functioning

Terms to Know:

Biological aging:

Psychological aging:

Sensory decline:

Social aging:

Disengagement theory:

Activity theory:

Continuity theory:

Impact of Aging Parents on Adult Children

Gerontology

Terms to Know:

Gerontology:

Geriatric social work practice:

Personality Theories

Hippocrates and his humors:

Human Development, Diversity and Behavior in the Environment

William Sheldon

Body type theories:

- _____
  _____

- _____
  _____

- _____
  _____

Gordon Allport

_____
_____
_____
_____

Carl Rogers

_____
_____
_____
_____

Theories of Conflict

Words to know:
Conflict theories:
_____
_____
_____
Marxism:
_____
_____
_____

Karl Marx (1818-1883)

_____
_____
_____
_____

Ludwig Gumplowicz (1838-1909)

_____
_____
_____
_____
_____

C. Wright Mills (1916-1952)

_____
_____
_____
_____

Factors Influencing Self-Image

Terms to Know:
Self-image:
_____
Self-esteem:
_____
Religion:
_____
_____
Spirituality:
_____
_____

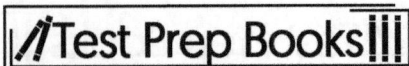

Human Development, Diversity and Behavior in the Environment

Benefits of being a spiritual person:

- _____
- _____
- _____
- _____
- _____

Self-image throughout the lifespan:

- Infancy: _____
- Childhood: _____
- Adolescence: _____

- Adulthood: _____

Impact of disability on self-image:
_____

Effects of trauma on self-image:
_____

Body Image

Body image:
_____

Factors associated with persistent negative body image:

- _____
- _____
- _____
- _____

Human Development, Diversity and Behavior in the Environment

- _____
- _____

Parenting Skills and Capacities

Four styles of parenting:

- _____
- _____
- _____
- _____

Addiction and Substance Use

_____

Feminist Theory

_____

Influential feminist theorists:
- **Anna Freud (1895-1982)**
- **Jean Baker Miller (1927-2006)**
- **Carol Tavris (1944-)**
- **Nancy Chodorow (1944-)**
- **Harriet Lerner (1944-)**
- **Carol Gilligan (1936-)**

Human Development, Diversity and Behavior in the Environment

- **Gail Sheehy (1937-2020)**

Out of Home Placement

Human Genetics

Social work practice skills related to genetics:

-
-
-
-
-

Social work values related to genetics:

-
-
-

-
-

Family Life Cycle

Family life cycle theories:

Common conceptualization of the life cycle stages:

-
-
-
-
-
-

Human Development, Diversity and Behavior in the Environment

Family Dynamics and Functioning

Family dynamics:

Common influences on family dynamics:

-
-
-
-
-

Common roles in the family that may result from particular family dynamics:

-
-
-

Theories of Couples' Development

Stages of long-term relationships:

-
-
-
-
-

Dr. Susan Campbell

Campbell's five stages of couples' development:

-
-
-
-
-

Impact of Physical and Mental Illness on Family Dynamics

Psychological Defense Mechanisms

Terms to Know:

Freud's psychoanalytic theory:

Defense mechanisms:

Types of defense mechanisms:

Repression:

Displacement:

Sublimation:

Rationalization:

Reaction formation:

Denial:

Projection:

Addiction Theories and Concepts

Terms to Know:

Moral Model:

Disease model, or medical model of addiction:

Biopsychosocial model of addition:

Learning theory of addiction:

Human Development, Diversity and Behavior in the Environment

Genetic theory:
_____
_____
_____
_____
_____

Systems and Ecological Perspectives and Theories

Terms to Know:

Systems Theory:
_____
_____
_____

Microsystems:
_____
_____
_____

Mesosystems:
_____
_____
_____

Macrosystems:
_____
_____
_____

Ecological systems perspective:
_____
_____
_____

Common interventions based on systems theory:

- _____
  _____

- _____
  _____

- _____
  _____

Role Theories
_____
_____
_____
_____
_____
_____

Theories of Group Development and Functioning

Potential methods for planning interventions:

- _____
  _____

- _____
  _____

- _____
  _____

- _____
  _____

- _____
  _____

- _____
- _____

The process of group therapy:
_____
_____
_____
_____

Theories of Social Change and Community Development

Community development theory:
_____
_____
_____

Community-level change:
_____
_____
_____

Interpersonal Relationships
_____
_____
_____
_____
_____

Strengths-Based and Resilience Theories

Strengths perspective:
_____
_____
_____

Resilience theories:
_____
_____
_____

Impact of Stress, Trauma, and Violence

Common trauma responses:

- _____
_____
_____
_____

- _____
_____
_____

- _____
_____
_____

- _____
_____
_____

- _____
_____
_____

- _____
_____
_____

- _____
_____
_____

- _____
- _____

Common Effects of Stress

Body:
_____

Mood:
_____

Behavior:
_____

Symptoms for the consideration of a PTSD diagnosis:

- _____
- _____
- _____

- _____

Crisis Intervention Theories

Crisis intervention:
_____

Gerald Caplan
_____

Caplan's Stages of Crises

Stage 1:
_____

Stage 2:
_____

Stage 3:
_____

Stage 4:
_____

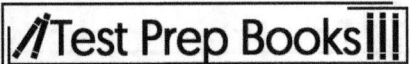

Human Development, Diversity and Behavior in the Environment

The Crisis Intervention Process

Engage and Asses:

Set Goals and Implement Treatment:

Evaluate and Terminate:

Theories of Trauma-Informed Care

Impact of the Environment

Impact of physical environment

Person-in-environment (PIE) theory:

Impact of Political Environment and examples:

-
-
-
-

Impact of Social Environment

-

Human Development, Diversity and Behavior in the Environment

- _____
- _____
- _____
- _____

Impact of Economic Changes

- _____
- _____
- _____

- _____
- _____
- _____

Impact of Culture Environment

Terms to Know:

Race: _____

Ethnic identity: _____

William Cross

_____

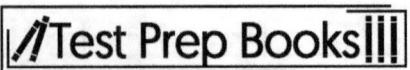

Human Development, Diversity and Behavior in the Environment

William Cross's Stages of Identity Development:

- _____
  _____
  _____
  _____

- _____
  _____
  _____
  _____

- _____
  _____
  _____
  _____

- _____
  _____
  _____
  _____

- _____
  _____
  _____
  _____

<u>Derald Sue and David Sue</u>

_____
_____
_____

Sue and Sue's Stages of Racial/Cultural Identity Development:

- _____
  _____
  _____
  _____

- _____
  _____
  _____
  _____

- _____
  _____
  _____
  _____

- _____
  _____
  _____

- _____
  _____
  _____

Human Development, Diversity and Behavior in the Environment

Life Events, Stressors, and Crises on Individuals, Families, Groups, Organizations, and Communities

Terms to Know:

Life events:

Reuben Hill's ABCX Model:

Positive coping mechanisms:

Negative coping strategies:

Person-In-Environment (PIE) Theory

Carl Germain

Terms to Know:

Life stress:

Adaptation:

Coping:

Power:

Human Relatedness:

Communication Theories and Styles

Terms to Know:

Niklas Luhmann's Theory:

Autopoiesis:

The Shannon and Weaver model of communication:

The Berlo model of communication:

Passive communication:

Passive communicators:

Human Development, Diversity and Behavior in the Environment

Aggressive communicators:

Passive-aggressive communication:

Passive-aggressive communicators:

Assertive communication:

Assertive communicators:

Psychoanalytic and Psychodynamic Approaches

Psychodynamic approaches:

Carl Jung

Jung's theory:

Jung's two parts of the unconscious:

Personal unconscious:

Collective unconscious (transpersonal):

Jung's four main archetypes of the collective unconscious:

Persona:

Anima/animas:

Shadow:

Self:

Loss, Separation, and Grief

Terms to Know:
Concept of loss:
Separation:
Grief:

Elisabeth Kubler-Ross's five stages of grief:

Concepts of Abuse and Neglect

Terms to Know:

Physical abuse:

Neglect:

Abuse and Neglect Throughout the Lifespan

Sexual abuse:

Indicators of child sexual abuse:

-
-
-
-
-
-
-

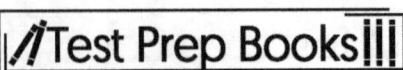

Human Development, Diversity and Behavior in the Environment

- _____
- _____
- _____
- _____
- _____
- _____
- _____
- _____

Terms to Know:

Psychological abuse:
_____
_____

Physical abuse:
_____
_____

Physical neglect:
_____
_____

Effects of Physical, Sexual, and Psychological Abuse

_____
_____
_____
_____

_____
_____

Exploitation Across the Lifespan and Perpetrators of Abuse, Neglect and Exploitation

Terms to Know:

Exploitation:
_____
_____

Financial exploitation:
_____
_____

Sexual exploration:
_____
_____
_____

Abuse perpetrators:
_____
_____
_____

Diversity, Social/Economic Justice, and Oppression

Effects of Disability on Biopsychosocial Functioning Throughout the Lifespan

_____
_____
_____

Human Development, Diversity and Behavior in the Environment

Biopsychosocial model:

Effects of Culture, Race, and Ethnicity on Behaviors, Attitudes, and Identity

Theory of learned helplessness:

Effects of Discrimination and Stereotypes on Behaviors, Attitudes, and Identity

Terms to Know:

Discrimination:

Direct discrimination:

Indirect discrimination:

Harassment:

Secondary victimization:

Influence of Sexual Orientation and Impact of Transgender and Transitioning Process on Behaviors, Attitudes, and Identity

Terms to Know:

Sexual orientation:

Conversion theory:

Systemic Discrimination

Systemic (institutionalized) discrimination:

Examples of systemic discrimination:

-
-
-

Human Development, Diversity and Behavior in the Environment

Culturally Competent Social Work Practice

What is required of social workers according to the NASW Code of Ethics:

- _____

- _____

- _____

- _____

- _____

- _____

Gender, Gender Identity, and Sexual Orientation Concepts

Terms to Know:

Gender:
_____

Gender identity:
_____

Sexual orientation:
_____

Sexual preference:
_____

Types of sexual orientation:

Types of gender identity:

- _____

- _____

- _____

Social and Economic Justice

Words to know

Social justice:
_____

38

NASW Code of Ethics:

Globalization:

Effects of Poverty:

Criminal Justic Systems:

Assessment and Intervention Planning

Biopsychosocial History and Collateral Data

Terms to Know:

Holistic assessment:
_____
_____
_____

Biopsychosocial framework:
_____
_____
_____

Identification:
_____
_____
_____
_____

Chief complaint:
_____
_____
_____
_____

Social development:
_____
_____

History:
_____
_____
_____
_____
_____

Presenting problem:
_____
_____
_____
_____

Past Personal:
_____
_____
_____
_____

Medical:
_____
_____
_____
_____

Mental Health:
_____
_____

Assessment and Intervention Planning

_____

_____

Substance Use:

_____

_____

_____

_____

Mental Status Examination

_____

_____

_____

_____

_____

_____

Biopsychosocial Responses to Illness and Disability

_____

_____

_____

_____

_____

Biopsychosocial Factors Related to Mental Health

Biopsychosocial model:

_____

_____

_____

_____

1. _____ factors:

_____

_____

_____

_____

2. _____ factors:

_____

_____

_____

_____

3. _____ factors:

_____

_____

_____

_____

Psychosocial Stress

_____

_____

_____

Indicators of psychosocial stress:

- _____

- _____

- _____

- _____

- _____

- _____

- _____

- _____

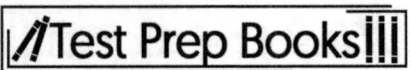

- _____
- _____
- _____

Basic Medical Terminology

The Cardiovascular System:
_____
_____
_____

Related terms:
- _____
- _____
- _____
- _____
- _____
- _____
- _____

The Digestive System:
_____
_____

Related terms:
- _____

- _____
- _____
- _____
- _____
- _____
- _____
- _____

The Endocrine System:
_____
_____
_____

Related terms:
- _____
- _____
- _____

The Integumentary System
_____
_____
_____

Related terms:
- _____
- _____

Assessment and Intervention Planning

- _____
- _____
- _____
- _____
- _____
- _____
- _____

The Lymphatic System

_____
_____
_____

Related terms:

- _____
- _____
- _____
- _____

The Musculoskeletal System:

_____
_____
_____

Related terms:

- _____

- _____
- _____
- _____
- _____
- _____
- _____
- _____

The Nervous System

_____
_____
_____

Related terms:

- _____
- _____
- _____
- _____
- _____

The Renal System:

_____
_____
_____

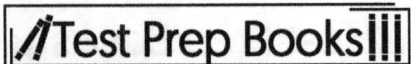

Related terms:

- _____
- _____
- _____
- _____
- _____
- _____
- _____
- _____

The Reproductive System:

_____
_____
_____

Related terms:

- _____
- _____
- _____
- _____
- _____
- _____
- _____

- _____
- _____
- _____
- _____

The Respiratory System:

_____
_____
_____

Related terms:

- _____
- _____
- _____
- _____
- _____
- _____
- _____

Mental and Emotional Illness Throughout the Lifespan

Symptoms of mental and emotional illness:

- _____

Assessment and Intervention Planning

- _____
- _____
- _____
- _____
- _____
- _____
- _____
- _____
- _____
- _____
- _____
- _____
- _____
- _____
- _____

Information Available from Other Sources

Primary sources of information:
_____
_____
_____

Secondary sources of information:
_____
_____
_____

Obtaining Sensitive Information

Information sheet:
_____
_____
_____

Presenting problems:
_____
_____
_____

Principle 1:
_____
_____

Key points:

- _____
  _____

- _____
  _____

- _____
  _____

Principle 2:
_____
_____

Technique:
_____
_____
_____
_____

Principle 3:
_____
_____
_____

Technique:

Principle 4:

Question Techniques:

Note Taking Techniques:

Indicators of Addiction and Substance Use

-
-
-
-
-

-
-

Indicators of Somatization

Co-Occurring Disorders and Condition

Signs that a co-occurring disorder is present:

-

-

Assessment and Intervention Planning

_____
_____
_____
_____
_____

Symptoms of Neurologic and Organic Disorders

_____
_____
_____

Symptoms include:

- _____
- _____
- _____
- _____
- _____
- _____
- _____
- _____

Indicators of Sexual Dysfunction

_____
_____
_____

- _____
- _____
- _____
- _____
- _____
- _____
- _____
- _____

Methods Used to Assess Trauma

Trauma:

_____
_____
_____
_____
_____

Traumatic Stress and Violence

Indicators of traumatic stress and violence include:

- _____
- _____
- _____
- _____
- _____
- _____

Assessment and Intervention Planning

- _____
- _____
- _____
- _____

Psychotropic and Non-Psychotropic Prescription and Over-the-Counter Medications

Psychotropic prescription medications:
_____
_____
_____
_____
_____

Non-psychotropic prescription medications:
_____
_____
_____
_____
_____

Assessment Methods and Techniques

Problem Formulation

Problem system:
_____
_____
_____
_____
_____

Three key areas to address when reviewing the problem history:

- Onset:
  _____
  _____
  _____
  _____

- Progression:
  _____
  _____
  _____
  _____

- Severity:
  _____
  _____
  _____
  _____

  o _____
  o _____
  o _____
  o _____
  o _____
  o _____

Psychosocial Stressors

Assessment and Intervention Planning

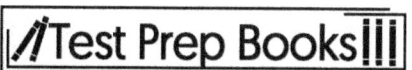

Terms to Know:

Likert Scale:

Life Events Scale:

ABCS of a problem:

Antecedents:

Behaviors:

Consequences:

Involving Clients/Client Systems in Problem Identification

Techniques and Instruments used to Assess Clients/Client Systems

Most common tests:

- Beck Depression Inventory-II (BDI-II):

- Bricklin Perceptual Scales (BPS):

- Millon instruments:
  -
  -
  -
  -

- Minnesota Multiphasic Personality Inventory (MMPI-2):

- Myers-Briggs Type Indicator:

- Quality of Life Inventory (QOLI):

Assessment and Intervention Planning

- Thematic Apperception Test (TAT):

- Rorschach Test:

- Wechsler Adult Intelligence Scale-Fourth Edition (WAIS-IV):

Incorporating Psychological and Educational Tests into Assessment

Risk Assessment Methods

-

-

-

Client's Danger to Self and Other

Obvious or discreet indicators:

-
-
-
-
-
-

Risk factors for Danger to Self and Others

-

Assessment and Intervention Planning

Risk Factors Related to Suicide

Assessment and Intervention Planning

- _____
- _____
- _____
- _____
- _____
- _____
- _____
- _____
- _____

Assessing the Client's/Client System's Strengths, Resources, and Challenges

Internal support systems:
_____
_____
_____

Dual perspective worksheet:
_____
_____
_____

Assessing Motivation, Resistance, and Readiness to Change
_____
_____
_____

Indicators of high motivation and low resistance:

- _____
- _____

- _____
- _____

Indicators of low motivation and high resistance:

- _____
- _____
- _____

Assessing the Client's/Client System's Communication Skills
_____
_____
_____

Assessing the Client's/Client System's Coping Abilities
_____
_____
_____

Terms to Know:

Client system:
_____
_____

Avoidance pattern:
_____
_____
_____

Assessment and Intervention Planning

Strengths and Challenges of the Client

Terms to Know:

Individual client strengths:
_____
_____
_____

Client's system:
_____
_____
_____

Client challenges:
_____
_____
_____

Assessing Ego Strengths

Ego strength:
_____
_____
_____

Positive or high ego strength is marked by:

- _____
- _____
- _____
- _____
- _____
- _____
- _____

Placement Options Based on Assessed Level of Care

_____
_____
_____
_____
_____
_____
_____

Diagnostic and Statistical Manual of the American Psychiatric Association

_____
_____
_____
_____
_____
_____
_____

Notable changes to the *DSM-5-TR* as of 2022:

- _____
- _____
- _____
- _____
- _____

Assessment and Intervention Planning

- _____
  _____
- _____
  _____
- _____
  _____
- _____
  _____
- _____
  _____

DSM-5-TR diagnostic criteria chapters:

- _____
- _____
- _____
- _____
- _____
- _____
- _____
- _____
- _____
- _____

- _____
  _____
- _____
  _____
- _____
  _____
- _____
  _____
- _____
  _____
- _____
  _____
- _____
  _____
- _____

Indicators of Behavioral Dysfunction and Crisis Plans

Terms to Know:

"Four Ds" of Abnormality:
_____
_____
_____

Deviant behavior:
_____
_____
_____

Dysfunction:
_____
_____
_____

Distress:
_____
_____
_____

Assessment and Intervention Planning

Danger:

Duration (5th D):

Crisis:

Objective and Subjective Data

Subjective data:

Objective data:

SOAP method:

BIRP documentation method:

Methods to Interpret and Communicate Policies and Procedures

Factors in policy and procedure development:

-
-
-

Factors to consider when evaluating the effectiveness of policies and procedures:

-
-
-
-
-
-

Research Designs and Methods; Data Collection and Analysis Methods; Reliability and Validity in Social Work Research

Terms to Know:

Basic research:

Applied research:

Qualitative data methods:

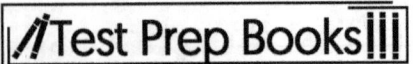

Assessment and Intervention Planning

Quantitative methods:

Correlational design:

Causal comparative design:

Experimental design:

Mixed research designs:

Qualitative data:

Quantitative data:

Reliability:

Inter-rater reliability:

Test-retest reliability:

Parallel forms reliability:

Internal consistency reliability:

Validity:

Face validity:

Construct validity:

Criterion validity:

Formative validity:

Sampling validity:

Intervention Planning

Methods to Involve Clients in Intervention Planning

Indicators of Motivation, Resistance, and Readiness to Change

Resistance:

Six stages of readiness to change:

-
-
-
-
-
-

Cultural Considerations in the Creation of an Intervention Plan

Intervention/Treatment Modalities

Things to consider when constructing interventions or treatment modalities:

-
-
-
-
-
-

Intervention, Treatment, and Service Plans

_____
_____
_____

Psychotherapies

_____
_____

Impact of Immigration, Refugee, or Undocumented Status on Service Delivery

_____
_____
_____
_____
_____

Discharge, Aftercare, and Follow-Up Planning

_____
_____
_____

Discharge planning:
_____
_____

The discharge summary should:
- _____
- _____

- _____
- _____
- _____
- _____
- _____
- _____
- _____
- _____
- _____
- _____

Follow-up Techniques in Social Work

_____
_____
_____

Interventions with Clients/Client System

Intervention Processes and Techniques for Use Across Systems

Interviewing Techniques

- _____
- _____
- _____
- _____
- _____

Methods of Summarizing Communication

Methods of Facilitating Communication

Using Bias-Free Language in Interviewing

Phases of Interventions and Treatment

Four Stages of the Treatment intervention process

- _____
- _____
- _____
- _____

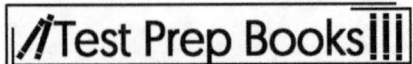

Interventions with Clients/Client System

Problem-Solving Models and Approaches

- _____
- _____
- _____
- _____

Engaging and Motivating Clients/Client Systems

Non-voluntary clients:
_____

Engaging and Working with Involuntary Clients/Client Systems
_____

Obtaining and Providing Feedback
_____

Factors to consider when obtaining feedback from clients:

- _____
- _____
- _____
- _____

Factors to consider when receiving feedback during supervision/consultation:

- _____
- _____

Active Listening and Observation

Nonverbal behaviors:
_____

Interventions with Clients/Client System

Verbal and Nonverbal Communication Techniques

Congruence in Communication

Limit-Setting Techniques

Role-Play Techniques

Role-Modeling Techniques

Types of modeling:

-
-

-

-

Harm Reduction for Self and Others

Teaching Coping and Other Self-Care Skills to Clients

Client Self-Monitoring Techniques

Methods of Conflict Resolution

Metacommunication:

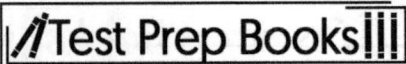

Interventions with Clients/Client System

Crisis Intervention and Treatment Approaches

De-escalation:

Confrontation:

Trauma-Informed Care Systems:

Anger Management Techniques

Stress Management Techniques

Cognitive and Behavioral Interventions

> **Terms to Know:**
>
> Cognitive approaches:
>
> Cognitive distortions:
>
> Behavioral approaches:
>
> Cognitive behavioral therapies:

Strengths-Based and Empowerment Strategies and Interventions

Empowerment:

Client Contracting and Goal-Setting Techniques

> **Terms to Know:**
>
> Reciprocal goals:
>
> Shared goals:

Interventions with Clients/Client System

Contract:

Components of the contract:

Partializing Techniques

Assertiveness Training

Task-Centered Approaches

Task Centered Practice

Psychoeducation Methods

Group Work Techniques and Approaches

Group work:

Open groups:

Closed groups:

Classifications of the stages of group development:

-
-
-

Family Therapy Models, Interventions, and Approaches

Social workers must:

-

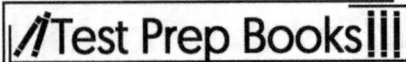

- _____
- _____
- _____

Terms to Know:

Boundaries:
_____
_____

Emotional Proximity and Distance:
_____
_____

Enmeshed:
_____
_____

Disengaged:
_____
_____

Family Hierarchy:
_____
_____

Homeostasis:
_____
_____

Alliances:
_____
_____
_____

Couples Interventions and Treatment Approaches

_____
_____
_____
_____
_____

Out-of-Home Displacement

_____
_____
_____
_____
_____

Permanency Planning

_____
_____
_____
_____
_____

Mindfulness and Complementary Therapeutic Approaches

Word to know:

Complementary therapeutic approaches:
_____

Interventions with Clients/Client System

Mindfulness: _____

Meditation: _____

Yoga: _____

Case Management

_____

Process of case management:

- _____
- _____
- _____
- _____
- _____

Follow-up Techniques

Follow-up session: _____

Case Presentation

_____

Measurable Objectives for Client System Intervention, Treatment, and Service Plans

SMART goals:

- S_____
- M_____
- A_____
- R_____
- T_____

Key recommendations:

- _____
- _____
- _____
- _____

- _____
  _____
  _____

Evaluating a Client's Progress
_____
_____
_____

Primary, Secondary, and Tertiary Prevention Strategies

Emphasis on Prevention in Social Work

Three Stages of Prevention

Three-stage model of prevention:
_____
_____

- _____
  _____

- _____
  _____
  _____

- _____
  _____
  _____

Client Readiness for Termination
_____
_____
_____

Workers should discuss the following when preparing clients for termination:

- _____
- _____
- _____
- _____
- _____

Methods, Techniques, and Instruments Used to Evaluate Social Work Practice
_____
_____
_____

Interventions with Clients/Client System

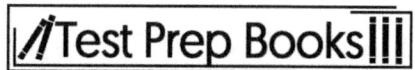

Evidence-Based Practice and Dissemination of Findings

___

Terms to Know:

Independent variable:
___

Dependent variable:
___

Randomized controlled trial (RCT):
___

Reliability:
___

Validity:
___

External validity:
___

Internal validity:
___

Case Recording for Practice Evaluation or Supervision

___

Health Insurance Portability and Accountability Act of 1996 (HIPAA):
___

Consultation Approaches

___

Interdisciplinary and Intradisciplinary Team Collaboration

___

Basic Terminology of Other Professions

___

Case Recording, Documentation, and Management of Practice Records

_____
_____
_____
_____
_____
_____

Intervention Processed and Techniques for Use with Larger Systems

Methods to Establish Program Objectives and Outcomes

Logic model:
_____
_____
_____

Availability of Community Resources

_____
_____
_____
_____
_____
_____

Methods of Service Delivery

- _____
  _____
  _____

- _____
  _____
  _____

- _____
  _____
  _____

- _____
  _____
  _____

Methods of Advocacy for Policies, Services, and Resources to Meet Client Needs

_____
_____
_____

Policies and Procedures that Minimize Risk for Individuals, Families, Groups, Organizations, and Communities

_____
_____
_____
_____
_____
_____

Interventions with Clients/Client System

___
___
___

Social Policy Development and analysis

___
___
___
___

Organizational and Social Policy

Types of societal influences that can affect social policy:

- ___
- ___
- ___
- ___
- ___

• ___
___
___

Formal Documents

___
___
___
___
___
___
___
___

Service Networks or Community Resources

___
___
___

Community Organizing and Social Planning Methods

Social change process:

- ___
- ___
- ___
- ___

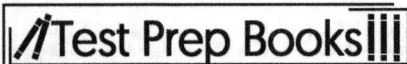

- _____

Methods of Networking

_____
_____
_____
_____
_____

Mobilizing Community Participation

_____
_____
_____
_____
_____

Governance Structures

_____
_____
_____
_____
_____

Organizational Development and Structure

_____
_____
_____
_____
_____

Effects of Policies, Procedures, Regulations, and Legislation on Social Work Practice and Service Delivery

_____
_____
_____
_____

Policies must address:

- _____
- _____
- _____
- _____
- _____

Quality Assurance

Terms to Know:
Quality assurance: _____ _____
Program assessments and social worker evaluations: _____ _____
Benchmarks: _____ _____
Auditing: _____ _____

Interventions with Clients/Client System

Impact of the Political Environment on Policy-Making

_____
_____
_____

Significant Social Welfare Legislation:

- _____
- _____
- _____
- _____
- _____
- _____
- _____

Leadership and Management Techniques

_____
_____
_____
_____
_____

Fiscal Management Techniques

_____
_____
_____
_____

_____
_____

Educational Components, Techniques, and Methods of Supervision

_____
_____
_____
_____
_____
_____
_____

Terms to Know:

Visual techniques:
_____
_____

Listening techniques:
_____
_____

Hands-on techniques:
_____
_____

Learning Needs and Learning Objectives for Supervisees

_____
_____
_____
_____
_____

Interventions with Clients/Client System

Effect of Program Evaluation Findings on Services

_____
_____
_____
_____
_____
_____

Terms to Know:

Needs assessments:
_____
_____

Cost-effectiveness:
_____

Cost-benefit analysis:
_____
_____
_____

Outcomes assessments:
_____
_____
_____

Techniques Used to Evaluate a Client's Progress

_____
_____
_____
_____

Professional Relationships, Values, and Ethics

Professional Values and Ethical Issues

_____
_____
_____
_____
_____
_____
_____

Legal and Ethical Issues Related to the Practice of Social Work

_____
_____
_____
_____
_____
_____
_____

Six core purposes of the NASW Code of Ethics:

- _____
  _____
  _____

- _____
  _____
  _____
  _____

- _____
  _____
  _____

- _____
  _____
  _____

- _____
  _____
  _____
  _____

- _____
  _____
  _____

Professional Values and Principles

Terms to Know:

Values:
_____
_____
_____

Professional Relationships, Values, and Ethics

Moral foundations:
_____
_____
_____

Value conflict:
_____
_____
_____

Value suspension:
_____
_____
_____

Individual morality:
_____
_____
_____

The three main values in social work:

- _____
  _____
  _____
  _____

- _____
  _____
  _____
  _____

- _____
  _____
  _____
  _____

Ethical Dilemmas
_____
_____
_____
_____

NASW's steps that should be taken when attempting to resolve and ethical dilemma:

```
┌─────────────────────┐
└──────────┬──────────┘
           ▼
┌─────────────────────┐
└──────────┬──────────┘
           ▼
┌─────────────────────┐
└──────────┬──────────┘
           ▼
┌─────────────────────┐
└──────────┬──────────┘
           ▼
┌─────────────────────┐
└──────────┬──────────┘
           ▼
┌─────────────────────┐
└─────────────────────┘
```

Client Competence and Self-Determination
_____
_____
_____
_____

Professional Relationships, Values, and Ethics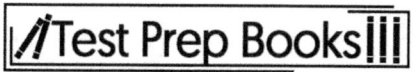

Protecting and Enhancing Client Self-Determination

Client's Right to Refuse Services

Professional Boundaries

Terms to Know:

Professional boundaries:

Conflicting values:

Vicarious trauma:

Rescuer role:

Personal boundary issues:

Potential boundary issues with clients:

-
-
-
-

Strategies for Setting and Maintaining Professional Boundaries in Social Work

- Strategy 1:
- Strategy 2:
- Strategy 3:

Professional Relationships, Values, and Ethics

- Strategy 4: _____

- Strategy 5: _____

- Strategy 6: _____

- Strategy 7: _____

Self-Disclosure

_____

Documentation

_____

NASW Code of Ethics guidelines for using client information for evaluation:

- _____

- _____

- _____

- _____

- _____

Termination

Termination: _____

Abandonment: _____

Death and Dying

_____

Research Ethics

_____

Professional Relationships, Values, and Ethics

Institutional Review Board (IRB):

Supervision and Consultation

Supervision and Management

Social Worker Safety

Supervisee's Role in Supervision

Factors to consider when receiving feedback during supervision/consultation:

-
-

Accreditation and Licensing Requirements

Council on Social Work Education (CSWE):

Professional Development Activities

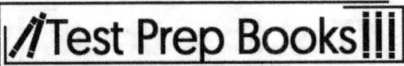

Confidentiality

Elements of Client Reports

_____
_____
_____
_____
_____

Obtaining Informed Consent

Informed consent form:
_____
_____
_____
_____
_____

Client Records

_____
_____
_____
_____
_____

Legal and Ethical Issues Regarding Confidentiality

_____
_____
_____
_____
_____

Mandatory Reporting

_____
_____
_____
_____
_____
_____
_____
_____

Mandatory reporting laws:
_____
_____
_____
_____

Impairment:
_____
_____
_____
_____

Professional Development and Use of Self

Components of the Social Worker-Client Relationship

_____
_____
_____

Professional Relationships, Values, and Ethics

Client's Role in the Problem-Solving Process

Social Worker's Role in the Problem-Solving Process

The problem-solving therapeutic model:

Roles and Responsibilities of the Social Worker and Client in the Intervention Process

Problem-solving approach to interventions:

-
-
-
-
-

Building and Maintaining a Helping Relationship

Rapport building:

Acceptance and Empathy in the Social Worker-Client Relationship

Empathy:

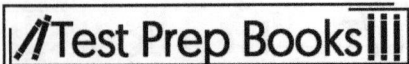

Professional Relationships, Values, and Ethics

Power and Transparency in the Social Worker-Client Relationship

_____
_____
_____

Transparency:
_____
_____
_____

Dual Relationships

_____
_____
_____
_____
_____

Boundary crossings:
_____
_____
_____

Boundary violation:
_____
_____
_____

Conditions in which a boundary crossing in unethical:

- _____

- _____

- _____

- _____

Transference and Countertransference in the Social Worker-Client Relationship

Transference:
_____
_____
_____

Countertransference:
_____
_____
_____

Impact of Domestic, Intimate Partner, and Other Violence on the Helping Relationship

_____
_____
_____
_____
_____
_____
_____

Diversity in the Social Worker-Client Relationship

Attitudes and Beliefs:
_____
_____

Knowledge:
_____
_____
_____

Cultural Skills:
_____
_____
_____

Professional Relationships, Values, and Ethics

Important techniques and strategies for working with various cultural and racial backgrounds:

- _____
- _____
- _____
- _____
- _____
- _____
- _____

Important techniques and strategies for working with various religious backgrounds:

- _____
- _____
- _____
- _____
- _____
- _____

Effect of Client's Developmental Level on the Social Worker-Client Relationship

Social Worker Self-Care Principles and Techniques

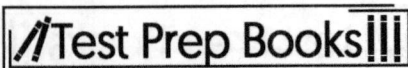

Burnout, Secondary Trauma, and Compassion Fatigue

_____
_____
_____
_____
_____
_____
_____
_____
_____

Safe and Positive Work Environment

_____
_____
_____
_____
_____

Professional Objectivity in the Social Worker-Client Relationship

_____
_____
_____
_____
_____

Influence of Social Worker's Own Values and Beliefs on the Social Worker-Client Relationship

_____
_____
_____
_____
_____
_____

Time Management Approaches

_____
_____
_____
_____

Transference and Countertransference Within Supervisory Relationships

_____
_____
_____
_____
_____
_____

Impact of Social Worker's Own Values and Beliefs on Interdisciplinary Collaboration

_____
_____

Dear ASWB Masters Test Taker,

Thank you for purchasing this study guide for your ASWB Masters exam. We hope that we exceeded your expectations.

Our goal in creating this study guide was to cover all of the topics that you will see on the test. We also strove to make our practice questions as similar as possible to what you will encounter on test day. With that being said, if you found something that you feel was not up to your standards, please send us an email and let us know.

We would also like to let you know about other books in our catalog that may interest you.

ASWB Masters

This can be found on Amazon: amazon.com/dp/1637752849

ASWB Clinical

amazon.com/dp/1637759460

We have study guides in a wide variety of fields. If the one you are looking for isn't listed above, then try searching for it on Amazon or send us an email.

Thanks Again and Happy Testing!
Product Development Team
info@studyguideteam.com

Online Resources

We host multiple bonus items online, including a customizable prep plan and a convenient study timer to help you manage your time. Scan the QR code or go to this link to access this content:

testprepbooks.com/online378/aswbmasters-fib

The first time you access the website, you will need to register as a "new user" and verify your email address.

If you have any issues, please email support@testprepbooks.com.

www.ingramcontent.com/pod-product-compliance
Lightning Source LLC
Chambersburg PA
CBHW080739230426

43665CB00020B/2801